ECDL.3

Module

for Microsoft Office 2000

Databases

ECDL3

for Microsoft Office 2000

Brendan Munnelly and Paul Holden

Databases

*Everything you need to pass the European
Computer Driving Licence®, module by module*

An imprint of **Pearson Education**

London · New York · Sydney · Tokyo · Singapore ·
Madrid · Mexico City · Munich · Paris

PEARSON EDUCATION LIMITED

Head Office:
Edinburgh Gate
Harlow CM20 2JE
Tel: +44 (0)1279 623623
Fax: +44 (0)1279 431059

London Office:
128 Long Acre
London WC2E 9AN
Tel: +44 (0)20 7447 2000
Fax: +44 (0)20 7240 5771
Website: www.it-minds.com

This edition published in Great Britain in 2002
First published in Great Britain in 2002 as part of *ECDL3 The Complete Coursebook for Microsoft Office 2000*

© Rédacteurs Limited 2002

ISBN 0-130-35462-7

British Library Cataloguing in Publication Data
A CIP catalogue record for this book can be obtained from the British Library

'European Computer Driving Licence' and ECDL and Stars device are registered trademarks of the European Computer Driving Licence Foundation Limited. Rédacteurs Limited is an independent entity from the European Computer Driving Licence Foundation Limited, and not affiliated with the European Computer Driving Licence Foundation in any manner.

This book may be used in assisting students to prepare for the European Computer Driving Licence examination. Neither the European Computer Driving Licence Foundation Limited, Rédacteurs Limited nor the publisher warrants that the use of this book will ensure passing the relevant examination.

Use of the ECDL-F approved Courseware logo on this product signifies that it has been independently reviewed and approved in complying with the following standards:

Acceptable coverage of all courseware content related to ECDL syllabus Module 5 version 3.0. This courseware material has not been reviewed for technical accuracy and does not guarantee that the end user will pass the associated ECDL examinations. Any and all assessment tests and/or performance based exercises contained in these Modular books relate solely to these books and do not constitute, or imply, certification by the European Driving Licence Foundation in respect of any ECDL examinations. For details on sitting ECDL examinations in your country please contact the local ECDL licensee or visit the European Computer Driving Licence Foundation Limited web site at http://www.ecdl.com.

References to the European Computer Driving Licence (ECDL) include the International Computer Driving Licence (ICDL).

ECDL Foundation Syllabus Version 3.0 is published as the official syllabus for use within the European Computer Driving Licence (ECDL) and International Computer Driving Licence (ICDL) certification programmes.

Rédacteurs Limited is at http://www.redact.ie

Brendan Munnelly is at http://www.munnelly.com

10 9 8 7 6 5 4 3 2 1

Typeset by Pantek Arts Ltd, Maidstone, Kent.
Printed and bound in Great Britain by Ashford Colour Press, Gosport, Hampshire.

The Publishers' policy is to use paper manufactured from sustainable forests.

Preface

The European Computer Driving Licence (ECDL) is an internationally recognized qualification in end-user computer skills. It is designed to give employers and job-seekers a standard against which they can measure competence – not in theory, but in practice. Its seven Modules cover the areas most frequently required in today's business environment. More than one million people in over fifty countries have undertaken ECDL in order to benefit from the personal, social and business advantages and international mobility that it provides.

In addition to its application in business, the ECDL has a social and cultural purpose. With the proliferation of computers into every aspect of modern life, there is a danger that society will break down into two groups – the information 'haves' and the information 'have nots'. The seven modules of the ECDL are not difficult, but they equip anyone who passes them to participate actively and fully in the Information Society.

The ECDL is not product-specific – you can use any hardware or software to perform the tasks in the examinations. And you can take the seven examinations in any order, and work through the syllabus at your own pace.

This book is one of a set of seven, each dealing with one of the ECDL modules. While each book can be used independently, if you are new to computers, you should read Module 2: *Using a computer and managing files* before attempting any of the other practical modules (such as this one). Module 2 teaches you the basic operations that are needed in the other practical modules.

The examples in these books are based on PCs (rather than Apple Macintoshes), and on Microsoft software, as follows:

- Operating system: Microsoft Windows 95/98
- Word Processing: Microsoft Word 2000
- Spreadsheets: Microsoft Excel 2000
- Databases: Microsoft Access 2000
- Presentations: Microsoft PowerPoint 2000
- Information and Communication: Microsoft Internet Explorer 5.0 and Microsoft Outlook Express 5.0

If you use other hardware or software, you can use the principles discussed in this book, but the details of operation will differ.

Welcome to the world of computers!

CONTENTS

Introduction

You can never be too rich, too healthy, or too informed. And the best kind of information to have is that which is organized in such a way that you can find the facts you need quickly and easily. It's also important to be able to store new items that you come across.

Databases – structured collections of facts about a particular topic – existed long before computers. Address books, card indexes and telephone directories are all examples of databases. But by storing your facts in a database file on a computer, you gain the power to manage and manipulate that information – even very large amounts of information – in a variety of ways.

You will discover how to view information in your database file from different perspectives, sort and select particular pieces you are interested in, and produce printed reports.

Think of this module as your chance to file rather than be filed. Good luck with it.

CHAPTER 1

What is a database?

In this chapter

A database, as you will learn in this chapter, is an organized collection of information relating to the same topic or subject matter. By 'organized' we mean that it should be easy to find a particular item of information in it, and to add new items to the database.

Microsoft Access is an application that enables you to create and work with databases. To give you an idea of what a computer database looks like, this chapter will take you on a tour of one of the sample databases provided with Access.

And by considering some examples of practical, everyday databases, you will gain an insight into the kind of decisions that designers need to make before they begin constructing their databases.

New skills

At the end of this chapter you should be able to:
- Explain what a database is
- List some common examples of databases
- State the advantages of computer databases over paper-based ones
- Start and quit Access
- Explore the sample databases provided with Access
- Explain two ways of looking at the information in a computer database
- Decide on a structure for a simple database

New words

At the end of this chapter you should be able to explain the following terms:
- Database
- Database management system (DBMS)
- Table
- Field
- Record
- Datasheet view
- Form view

An organized collection of information

database is a collection of information relating to the same topic or subject matter. It is usually organized in such a way that you can easily:

- Find the items of information you are interested in, and

- File away the new items that you come across.

Database
An organized collection of related information.

A database does not have to be kept on a computer. For example, address books, card indexes, and telephone directories are all databases (even though very few people would call them that!).

Storing a database on a computer, however, enables you to manipulate the information easily and quickly. For example, using a (paper-based) telephone directory, it is relatively easy to find a person's telephone number, but it is very difficult (but not impossible) to find the person's name if you only have their telephone number.

A computer-based directory enables you to find that information quickly and easily. You could also find the names of everyone who lives on a particular road, or everyone whose first name was 'Paul'. Or you could print a report showing the five most common surnames.

Computer-based databases are flexible: they enable you to deal with information – even very large quantities of information – in a variety of ways. Microsoft Access is an example of a database management system – an application that enables you to create and manage a database on a computer.

Database Management System (DBMS)

An application such as Microsoft Access that enables you to collect information on a computer, organize it in different ways, sort and select pieces of information of interest to you, and produce reports.

Records and fields

In a database, information is typically broken down into its smallest, most divisible parts. Each part goes into its own named field. For example, if you were entering names and addresses into a database, you would not put all the information into a single field, like this:

James Coogan Sweeney
10744 South Hoyne
Chicago
Illinois 60643
USA

You would normally enter each piece of information into a separate field, as follows:

FirstName	James
MiddleName:	Coogan
LastName:	Sweeney
FirstAddress:	10744 South Hoyne
SecondAddress:	
City:	Chicago
State:	Illinois
ZipCode:	60643
Country:	USA

Field

> *A single piece of information about a subject. More precisely, it is the space where that information is held.*

In a database, individual pieces of information (such as a telephone number) are called fields, and the set of information relating to one individual is called a record.

Record

> *One complete set of fields relating to the same subject.*

Tables and databases

A collection of records is called a table. If a database contains just a single table, the table is, in effect, the database. In this ECDL module you will be dealing only with single-table databases. All that you need know about multi-table databases is that Access allows you to create them.

When there are thousands or hundreds of thousands of records, a database management system comes into its own. A computer asked to extract and show only records where, for instance, surnames (LastName) begin with 's' and where postcodes (Zipcodes) begin with '60', responds at breathtaking speed, far beyond the capacity of human sorters.

A database management system, however, lacks 'common sense' – it is not able to make judgements. If you did not enter the information in the right field, it will not be retrieved correctly.

Table

A collection of records that contain the same fields. A database may contain one or more tables.

Two views: Datasheet and Form

With Access, and with most database management systems, you can view and manipulate information in two ways: in a datasheet, or in forms. In *Datasheet view*, you can see the information arranged in columns (one for each field) and rows (one for each record); it is similar in appearance to a spreadsheet.

Number	Bird Name	Colour	Number Seen	Migratory?	Size	Date Seen	Place Seen
1	Great Northern Diver	Black/White	23	☑	69		
2	Great Crested Grebe	Grey/White/Brown	21	☐	46	13/03/99	Dalkey
3	Little Grebe	Black/Brown	14	☐	24	04/09/98	Stephen's Green
4	Gannet	White/Black	5	☐	85	12/06/98	Ireland's Eye
5	Fulmar	White/Grey	3	☐	45		
6	Great Shearwater	White/Brown	7	☑	42		
7	Manx Shearwater	Black/White	17	☐	30		
8	Storm Petrel	Black/White	1	☐	13		
9	Cormorant	Black/White	3	☐	83	12/06/98	Ireland's Eye
10	Grey Heron	Grey/White	4	☐	90		
11	Mute Swan	White	12	☐	114	14/06/99	Malahide
12	Brent Goose	Black/White	34	☑	56	12/12/98	Dollymount
13	Greylag Goose	Grey	22	☑	76		
14	Shelduck	White/Brown/Black	16	☐	57		
15	Goldeneye	White/Black	9	☑	41		
16	Teal	Grey/Multicolour	14	☐	34	28/09/98	Wexford
17	Mallard	Green/White/Brown	16	☐	55	28/09/98	Wexford
18	Sparrowhawk	Blue/White	1	☑	28		
19	Kestrel	Grey/Brown	2	☐	33	27/09/98	Wexford
20	Pheasant	Red/Black	6	☐	53	08/08/81	Mauritius
22	Blue Tit	Blue/Yellow/Black/White	0	☐	6	07/06/99	Ballsbridge
(AutoNumber)			0	☐	0		

An example of Datasheet view, where you can see several records at once

Datasheet view

A view of a database table where you can see information presented in rows and columns, with several records visible at the same time.

A *Form view* presents all or selected information for a single record at a time. The form can be laid out in a format that is easier to read, perhaps with explanatory text. You can structure the form in such a way that it looks like a paper form, with the fields in the corresponding place on the screen.

An example of Form view, where you can see details from a single record only

Number	11
Bird Name	Mute Swan
Colour	White
Size	144
Migratory?	☐
Date Seen	Monday, June 14, 1999
Place Seen	Malahide

Form view

> *A view of a database table that presents all or selected information from a single record only.*

A good way of learning more about computer databases is by examining some sample ones. Access comes with three sample databases: Northwind, Orders, and Solutions. Exercise 1.1 takes you on a tour of the Northwind database. First, you need to start Access.

Starting Access

To start Access, either:

* Double-click on the Microsoft Access icon.

–or–

Microsoft
Access

* Choose **Start | Programs | Microsoft Access.**

Access starts and displays a dialog box that gives you the choice of opening an existing database, or of creating a new database.

Now let's take a tour of a database that Microsoft prepared earlier – the Northwind sample database.

Exercise 1.1: Opening the Northwind database

1   Select the Open an existing file option in the opening dialog box.

2 The sample databases may be listed in the dialog box: if they are, select Northwind.mdb.

If the sample databases are not listed, select the More Files item in the database list, and click OK. You can then navigate through the folders on your PC to find them. They are most likely to be in the following location:

C:\Program Files\Microsoft Office\Office\Samples

Use Windows Explorer or My Computer to find them if necessary. When you find Northwind.mdb, select it.

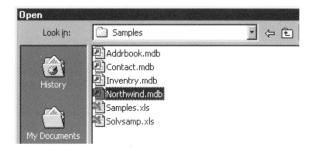

3 Click **Open**.

4 If you are presented with a welcome screen, click **OK** to close it.

Access now displays the Database window.

The Database window – the 'control centre' of Access
From here you can work with the various database objects.

Access file name extension

The file names of Access databases end in .mdb (Microsoft database). This helps you to distinguish Access files from other file types such as Excel spreadsheets (.xls) or Word documents (.doc).

The Database window

On the Database window you can see the following sections: Tables, Queries, Forms, Reports, Pages, Macros, and Modules. They are all sets of items – Access calls them *objects* – that are associated with the database in some way. For ECDL you need only learn about the first four: you don't need to worry about the ones named Pages, Macros and Modules.

- **Tables**: You will learn how to create a table in Chapter 2, and how to modify it in Chapter 3.

- **Queries**: Chapter 4 shows you how to create queries – predefined ways of viewing information from your table on screen.

- **Forms**: Chapter 5 shows you how to create and format the appearance of forms, and how to use them to enter and modify records.

- **Reports**: These enable you to extract information from your database as printouts. You will learn about reports in Chapter 6.

You will see the Database window a lot when you are working with Access. From here, you can open any of the database objects – to work with them or to change them – and when you are finished with that object, Access returns you to this Database window, from where you can work with any of the other objects easily.

When you first open a database, the Tables objects are normally on top. If not, simply click the Tables icon in the left frame of the dialog window.

Notice that the Northwind database contains several tables. Open Employees, either by selecting it and clicking **Open**, or by double-clicking on its name or icon. Have a look at the type of information it contains. This will give you a good idea of how databases are actually used.

- When a table, such as Employees, contains more fields than can be shown on a single screen, use the horizontal scroll bar to move right and left.

  If you scroll far enough to the right, you will see a Photo column. Double-click any one of these fields to view the employee's photo, and then close the photo window.

  If your horizontal scroll bar is not visible, you will have to click the Maximize button, after which the scroll bar becomes visible.

  Maximize button

  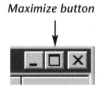

- When a table contains more records than can be shown on a single screen, use the vertical scroll bar to move up and down the range of records.

Database design considerations

In Chapter 2 you will create a database of your very own. But before using Access to build *any* database, take some time to think about the kind of information that you want to put into your database, and how you want to use it.

The following four examples demonstrate the kind of decisions that database designers need to make before they begin constructing their databases.

Example 1: the wine connoisseur's database

Henry is interested in wine. He reads the wine column in the newspapers and notes the recommendations. When he goes to the supermarket, he brings a list with him, so that he can select wine based on the recommendations. When he buys wine, he might have it in the house for some time before he tastes it, and he likes to record his impressions and compare notes with the original review.

Henry might include the following fields in his database:

- Wine Style (Red / White / Rosé / Sparkling / Sweet)
- Name
- Country/Region
- Grower
- Grape Varieties
- Vintage

- Available From (shop)
- Price
- Number Bought
- Date Bought
- Date Tasted
- Tasting Notes

- Recommended By
- Review Comments
- Buy Again?

With such a database, Henry could print out a separate list for each shop, he could list all the red wines, he could list all the white wines that cost less than £10, he could find where the wines by a particular grower were available, he could view the comments on different vintages of the same wine, and so on.

Example 2: the CD collector's database

Michelle plays the piano and has a large collection of CDs. When she is learning a new piece, she likes to listen to other people playing it. She has built a database with the following fields:

- CD Title
- Artist
- Track Number
- Name of Tune
- Composer
- Date Recorded

By sorting the database on the Name of Tune field, she can quickly identify the particular CDs that include the tune she is working on.

Example 3: the household manager's database

Oscar started his database for insurance purposes: it enabled him to build up a detailed record of his house contents. It included the following fields:

- Room
- Item
- Category
- Date Purchased
- Price Paid

With this database he was able to provide an accurate inventory to the insurance company to support a claim. He could provide the original cost, along with the depreciated value and the replacement value, based on the original cost and the elapsed time since the purchase. He could also quickly give a value for all the paintings in the house, the value of all the clothes in the upstairs rooms, or all the contents of a particular room.

Example 4: the bird watcher's database

Every weekend, Clara goes out with her field glasses and notebook, and spends some time watching birds. When she comes home, she puts details of what she has seen into a database. The database has the following fields:

- Bird Name
- Colour
- Size
- Number Seen
- Migratory?
- Place Seen
- Date Seen

Clara has entered into her database the basic information for the first five fields, based on her reference books, and she records her sightings every week. If she sees a bird that she is unable to identify, she can look up all birds of a certain colour and size. (Obviously this is not enough for identification, but it helps her find the right bird in her reference books.) She can then record the date and place of the sighting. After a while, she will be able to identify the best places and times of the year to spot the different species.

Thinking hard about fields

When you are deciding on the fields in the database, think carefully about how they are to be used. If, for example, you want to sort or select wines by country of origin, you should have a column for country: while you might know that Bordeaux is in France, Access doesn't. If you want to find all the albums produced by Nick Lowe, you have to record that information, and preferably in a consistent way (for example, last name followed by first name).

Go back and reread the example of Clara's bird spotting database – this is the database that you will build in Chapter 2.

Closing a database

To close an Access database, choose **File | Close**, or click the Close button on the Database window.

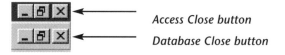

Access Close button
Database Close button

Quitting Access

To leave Access, choose **File | Exit**, or click the Close button on the Access window.

You have now completed Chapter 1 of the ECDL *Databases* module.

Chapter summary: so now you know

A *database* is a collection of information, typically held on a computer, and organized in such a way that you can find what you are looking for quickly and easily, and add new data as you need. Computer-based databases enable their users to manipulate large amounts of information more efficiently than paper-based ones.

Microsoft Access is an example of a *database management system* – an application that stores information on a computer, organizes it in different ways, sorts and selects pieces of information of interest to you, and produces reports.

A database holds at least one *table* of information; each table has a number of *records*; and each record has a number of *fields*. A field is a single piece of information about a subject. A record is one complete set of fields relating to the same subject. And a table is a collection of records. In single-table databases of the kind covered by this ECDL module, the table is the database.

The *Database window* is the 'control panel' of Access. Using its tabs, you can open and work with any of the application's *objects* including *Tables, Queries, Forms* and *Reports*.

Before building any database in Access, consider the information that you want to put into your database, and how you want to use it. Break it down into its smallest (and most useful) divisible parts – each such part should probably be a separate database field.

CHAPTER 2

Building your Access database

In this chapter

Get ready to build your first database in Access! This is not
as intimidating as it may sound. Access comes with a
number of samples that you can use as a basis for just about
any new database that you might want to create. So a lot of
the work is already done for you!

The decisions you need to make are: which sample table
is closest to the one I want? Which of its fields will I use?
And what new names will I give to the fields that I select?

Two new concepts you will meet in this chapter are keys
and indexes. The first is the unique identifier that makes
each record in your database different from all the others;
the second is a way of speeding up the sorting and retrieval
of records. You will also discover another way of looking at
your database, called Design view.

One aspect of database creation that Access cannot help
you with is data entry: only you can do that.

New skills

At the end of this chapter you should be able to:
- Start the Access Database Wizard
- Select a suitable sample table from the list provided
- Select from the sample table the fields you want in your table
- Rename the fields selected from the sample table to suit your needs
- Select a primary key to identify each of your records uniquely
- Enter data to a table in Datasheet view
- Adjust column width in Datasheet view
- Switch to and from Design view
- Create an index

New words

At the end of this chapter you should be able to explain the following terms:
- Database key
- Design view
- Database index

Overview of database creation

In this chapter you will create your first Access database. It will be similar to the one that Clara uses to record her bird-watching activities, as outlined in Chapter 1.

Access includes a Database Wizard to simplify the process of creating a database. You will use this automated feature to do some of the work, and you will do some of it the 'hard way', so that you will learn more about how the application works.

Database creation is a nine-step process:

> **Step one: Starting the Database Wizard**: You begin by starting the Access Database Wizard, and by naming and saving your new database. See Exercise 2.1.

> **Step two: Selecting your sample table**: Rather than create a new table from scratch, it is easier and faster to base it on one provided by Access. See Exercise 2.2.

> **Step three: Selecting your fields**: You probably won't want every field from the sample table included in your table, so you must specify which ones you need. See Exercise 2.3.

> **Step four: Renaming your fields**: Typically, you will need to rename at least some of the fields that you have selected from the sample table. This is the step at which you also name your table. See Exercise 2.4.

Step five: Setting your primary key: You need to tell Access which of your fields will act as the key field – the one that uniquely distinguishes each record from all the others. See Exercise 2.5.

Step six: Entering your data: You enter data to your new table in Datasheet view. See Exercise 2.6.

Step seven: Adjusting column width: In Datasheet view, some columns may be too narrow; others too wide. You need to know how to change column width. See Exercise 2.7.

Step eight: Switching to Design view: One further step to go, and you can perform it only after you switch from Datasheet view to Design view.

Step nine: Creating your index: An index greatly speeds up the sorting and retrieval of data. You create one in Exercise 2.8.

Ready? Let's go build a database.

You begin the creation of your new database by starting the Access Database Wizard.

Step one: starting the Database Wizard

Exercise 2.1: Starting the Access Database Wizard

1   How you create a database depends on whether or not Access is already open on your PC:

   • If Access is not already open, open it now. On the initial dialog box displayed, select Access database wizards, pages, and projects and then click **OK**.

- If Access is already open, click the File New button on the toolbar.

File New button

2 In the New dialog box, click the General tab, select the Database icon and click **OK**.

3 In the File New Database dialog box, give your new database a name – Birds.mdb – and indicate the folder in which you want to store it. By default, Access suggests that you save your databases in the My Documents folder. Accept or amend this location, as required.

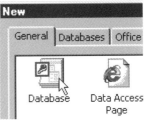

Database icon

4 Click the **Create** button.

   Access then displays the Database window.

5 Normally, when you create a database, the Table objects are shown on top in the Database window. If they are not, click the Tables icon.

Notice that, unlike the Northwind sample database, each of the object sets in the database you just created is empty. In this Chapter 2 you will create a table object; in Chapter 5, query and form objects. And in Chapter 6, a report object.

Step two: selecting your sample table

It would be impossible for anyone to anticipate precisely what you want to do with your database, so the Access Table Wizard offers you a wide range of choices.

In the next few exercises you will pick the options that come closest to matching your needs, and you will modify them until they are exactly what you want.

Exercise 2.2: Selecting a sample table

1   In the Tables view of the Database window, click the New Table button on the toolbar. Access displays the New Table dialog box.

New Table button

2   The New Table dialog box offers five ways to create a new table.

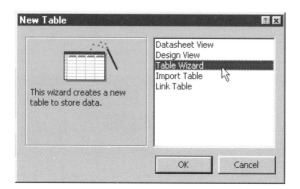

3   Select the Table Wizard option and click **OK.**

4   On the Table Wizard dialog box now displayed, you can see two option buttons – Business and Personal. Depending on which of these options you select, Access displays a different list of Sample Tables.

5   Select Business and browse through the Sample Tables list. For each table in the first list box, scroll through the sample fields in the second list box. None of the tables seems to be particularly appropriate for your needs.

6   Select the Personal option. Again, look through the sample tables. While there is nothing that relates specifically to bird-watching, one of the tables – Plants – could be modified to suit your bird-watching database.

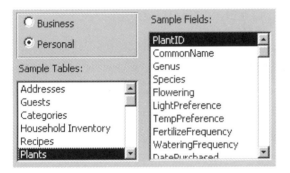

7   Select the Plants table – you will work with it in Exercise 2.3.

Step three: selecting your fields

The first screen of the Table Wizard shows three list boxes. The first displays Access's sample tables. (You selected the Plants table from this list in Exercise 2.2.) The second list shows all the fields supplied with the selected sample table. And the third list shows the fields that you have decided to include in your new table. Initially, the third list is empty.

To move a field from the Sample Fields box to the Fields in my new table box, click on it to select it, and then click the > button. If you change your mind about

Include selected field

Include all fields

Exclude selected field

Exclude all fields

a particular field, select it in the right-hand box and click the < button. You can include all the sample fields by clicking the >> button. Or remove all the fields from the right-hand box by clicking the << button.

Exercise 2.3: Selecting the fields you need

1 Move the following fields from the Sample fields list to the Fields in my new table list: PlantID, CommonName, Genus, Flowering, WateringFrequency, DatePurchased and PlacePurchased.

   When finished, the dialog box should look as shown.

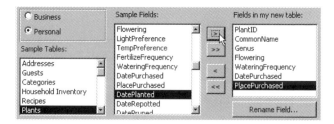

Step four: renaming your fields

Now that you have selected the fields you want to use from the
Wizard's sample table, your next task is to give them names
suitable for your new table. To rename a field, click on it in the
Fields in my new table list and click the **Rename Field** button.
You then type the new name for the field in the Rename Field
dialog box. Rename your fields as shown in Exercise 2.4.

Exercise 2.4: Renaming your fields

1 In the Fields in my new table list, select Plant ID. Click
the **Rename Field** button.

2 In the Rename Field dialog box, type the new name for
the field: Number. Click **OK**.

3 Repeat for the other fields in your new table, as follows:

Old Name	New Name
CommonName	Bird Name
Genus	Colour
Flowering	Migratory?
WateringFrequency	Size
DatePurchased	Date Seen
PlacePurchased	Place Seen

4 Click the **Next** button.

Congratulations! You have just created your first
Access table.

5 Now you have to give it a name.

What do you want to name your table?

Birds

Apply all your imagination: call your table Birds – the same name as the database that contains it.

In the same dialog box, Access asks you whether you want the Wizard to set a primary key, or whether you want to do it yourself. Okay, let's talk about keys.

Step five: setting your primary key

In the telephone directory there are many people listed with the surname Murphy; a number of them share the same first name, John. To find the one you want, you need some more information: where do they live? Even that might not be enough – father and son might have the same name and you might have to ask them some further questions to confirm that you are talking to the right one.

Well, in a computer system, that obviously is not satisfactory. Access needs to know which John Murphy you mean. And you don't want to send a bill, or, worse still, a cheque to the wrong John Murphy. So you give each record an identifier, called a key, which is unique to that record – it is not shared with any other. Exercise 2.5 takes you through the steps.

Database key

A field (or combination of fields) in a database record that is used to identify that record uniquely.

Exercise 2.5: Setting a primary key

1   On the second Table Wizard screen, having specified a name for your new table (in Exercise 2.4), select the option 'No, I'll set the primary key' and click the **Next** button.

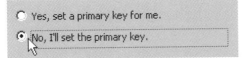

2 In answer to the question 'What field will hold data that is unique for each record', select 'Number'. (It should be already selected as the default.)

What field will hold data that is unique for each record?
Number

In answer to the question 'What type of data do you want the primary key to contain?', select 'Consecutive numbers Microsoft Access assigns automatically to new records'.

Consecutive numbers Microsoft Access assigns automatically to new records.

3 Click the **Next** button.

You have now defined your own primary key for your table.

4 Access then asks: what do you want to do next – modify the table design, enter data directly into the table, or enter data into a table using a form wizard?

Well, a table with no data is pretty boring, so you probably want to enter data directly into the table without further delay. Choose that option.

Enter data directly into the table.

5 Click the **Finish** button.

Step six: entering data in your table

When you create a new table, Access displays the table initially in Datasheet view as follows:

- Along the top are column headings that show your field names.

- Underneath the column headings is a single, blank row.

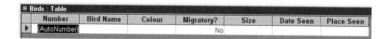

Birds : Table						
Number	Bird Name	Colour	Migratory?	Size	Date Seen	Place Seen
(AutoNumber)			No			

Click in any field: you can then enter data in that field. You can move from field to field using the Tab key or the arrow keys. There is an exception: the Number field (your primary key) is automatically assigned by Access – you cannot enter a new number or change an existing one. You will learn more about this feature in Chapter 3.

As soon as you start entering data for a record, a new line opens up underneath. So, no matter how many records you enter, there is always a blank record at the end where you can enter the next one.

Exercise 2.6: Entering data in your table

1   In the Birds table, fill in the details of a number of birds in the Bird Name, Colour, Migratory?, and Size fields as shown.

Number	Bird Name	Colour	Migratory?	Size
1	Great Northern Diver	Black/White	Yes	69
2	Great Crested Grebe	Grey/White/Brown	No	46
3	Little Grebe	Black/Brown	No	24
4	Gannet	White/Black	No	85
5	Fulmar	White/Grey	No	45
6	Great Shearwater	White/Brown	Yes	42
7	Manx Shearwater	Black/White	No	30
8	Storm Petrel	Black/White	No	13
9	Cormorant	Black/White	No	83
10	Grey Heron	Grey/White	No	90
11	Mute Swan	White	No	114
12	Brent Goose	Black/White	Yes	56
13	Greylag Goose	Grey	Yes	76
14	Shelduck	White/Brown/Black	No	57
15	Goldeneye	White/Black	Yes	41
16	Teal	Grey/Multicolour	No	34
17	Mallard	Green/White/Brown	No	55
18	Sparrowhawk	Blue/White	Yes	28
19	Kestrel	Grey/Brown	No	33
20	Pheasant	Green/Gold	No	0
21	Dodo	Blue/White/Yellow	No	90
22	Blue Tit	Blue/Yellow/Black/White	No	6
* (AutoNumber)			No	

At this stage, some fields may be too small to display all the information you enter: don't worry – you will learn how to adjust column width in Exercise 2.7.

In the case of Migratory?, if the fields contain checkboxes, you indicate that a bird is migratory by clicking on the checkbox. If the fields contain 'No' instead, you indicate that a bird is migratory by typing 'Yes' in the place of 'No'.

2 Close your table by clicking the lower Close button on the top right of the table (not the Access!) window. Access asks you if you want to save changes to the layout of the table. Click **Yes**.

3 Access returns you to the Database window, this time with one important difference: the new table you created – Birds – is shown on the Tables section.

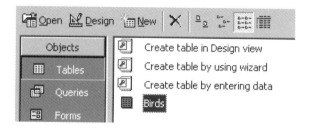

That's it. Now you know how to create a table in Access, and how to enter data into it in Datasheet view. (You will learn about entering data in Form view in Chapter 5.)

Step seven: changing the width of your columns

This is easy. By now you will have noticed that Access starts off by making all the columns the same width. Some of them are too narrow for their contents to be displayed in full (as, for example, in some of the birds' names).

And some columns are too wide: the datasheet takes up more space than necessary, with the result that some of your data may be pushed off the right of the screen, and you have to use the horizontal scroll bar to see it.

To change the width of a column, click on the dividing line (known as the *field delimiter*) between its title and the one to its right.

Bird Name ✛   Colour

Drag left or right to adjust the width of columns

Notice that the shape of the cursor changes. Then drag the cursor left or right until the column is the right size.

You can make the column width adjust automatically to fit the longest entry in the column by *double-clicking* on the field delimiter.

Exercise 2.7: Adjusting column width

1 On the Database window, double-click the Birds table to open it.

Bird Name		Bird Name
Great Northern		Great Northern Diver
Great Crested (		Great Crested Grebe
Little Grebe		Little Grebe
Gannet		Gannet
Fulmar		Fulmar
Great Shearwat		Great Shearwater
Manx Shearwat		Manx Shearwater
Before		*After*

2 Change the width of the Bird Name and Colour columns in the Birds table to improve the overall appearance of the table.

Step eight: switching to Design view

In Chapter 1, you were introduced to two views of a database: Datasheet view, where you can see several records arranged in rows and columns, and Form view, where you can see only a single record at a time. In Exercise 2.6, you entered data to your table in Datasheet view.

Now meet a third view: *Design view*. This is the view in which you can change the organizational structure of your table.

Design View button
in Datasheet view

- If your table is open in Datasheet view, switch to Design view by choosing **View | Design View** or by clicking the Design View button on the toolbar.

- If your table is open in Design view, you can return from Design view to Datasheet view by choosing **View | Datasheet View** or by clicking the Datasheet View button on the toolbar.

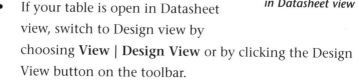

Datasheet View button
in Design view

The toolbar buttons enable you to switch quickly between the two views, so that when you make any design changes you can see their effect immediately.

If your table is not open, you can open it in Design view by selecting it at the Database window, and clicking the Design button.

Design View

> *A view in which you can change the organizational structure of your table. You create an index in Design View.*

Step nine: creating your index

Creating an index from one or more fields can greatly speed up the sorting and retrieval of records, particularly when databases become very large. Looking up a name in the index at the back of a book is easier than scanning hundreds of pages of text looking for it; a more sophisticated index might help differentiate between the 57 Smiths, possibly by including first names or addresses in the index.

Access can use table indexes to avoid time-wasting searches through thousands of records. A multiple-field index might, for example, be based on surname, first name and city, since searches are often based on these criteria.

Database index

> *A list of keys that a database can use to find and sort records. Indexes make such operations faster, as the database only needs to examine the index fields rather than entire records.*

Exercise 2.8 shows you how to build an index for your table.

Exercise 2.8: Creating an index

1   Display the Birds table in Design view.

2   Choose **View | Indexes** or click the Indexes
    button on the toolbar. You can see the indexes
    that are already set, each consisting of
    just one field.

Indexes button

3   In an empty row, type the following in the Index
    Name field:

    Where & When

4   Click anywhere in the Field Name column to the right of
    the text that you typed in Step 3. An arrow appears in
    the right of the field. Click on the arrow. From the drop-
    down list displayed, select Place Seen.

5   Click in the field beneath the one you used in Step 4
    and select   Date Seen.

6   Click in the field beneath the one you used in Step 5
    and select Bird Name.

7   Click the Close button at the top right of the Indexes
    dialog box, and then click the Close box at the top right
    of your Birds table.

8 When asked 'Do you want to save changes to the design of table Birds?', click **Yes**.

You have now set up a multiple-field index – the final step in the database creation checklist. You can now quit Access. You have completed Chapter 2 of the ECDL *Databases* module.

Chapter summary: so now you know

Access offers a *Database Wizard* that simplifies the process of creating a new database by providing a number of *sample tables*. Choose one that resembles the table that you want to create. You can customize your chosen sample table by selecting which of its fields you want to use, and then renaming the selected fields as required.

When you create a new table, Access displays it in Datasheet view, with *column headings* that show your selected field names above a single, blank row. You can type record data into the blank row. As soon as you enter one record, Access opens up a new line underneath, so that there is always a blank record at the end where you can enter the next one.

You can *change column width* manually at any stage, or make column width adjust automatically to the longest entry in the field.

A *key* is a field (or combination of fields) in a database record that uniquely identifies that record. An *index*, which you create in *Design view*, speeds up the sorting and retrieval of records.

You must *save* and *name* both the database and the table that the database contains.

CHAPTER 3

Modifying your Access database

In this chapter

Now that you have built your first database, you need to learn how to make changes to it. In this chapter you will discover how to remove records you no longer need from your database, and how to reorder existing ones.

Access allows you to add new fields to your records at any time, either at the end of a record or anywhere in the middle. But when you add new fields, you may need to go back and edit all records that you have already entered. So it makes sense to select your fields correctly at database design stage!

As you will also learn in this chapter, each field in a table has a particular data type that tells Access how to treat the field, how the data is to be stored, and what kind of data is allowed in it. Ideally, you should select the correct data type for each field before you enter data, because changing a field's data type at a later stage may result in data loss.

Access offers a searchable online help system that you can access in two ways: from the Help menu, and from the question mark button at the top right of individual dialog boxes.

New skills

At the end of this chapter you should be able to:
- Edit the contents of a field
- Delete a record
- Know when to use the following data types: Text, Memo, Number, Date/Time, Currency, AutoNumber and Yes/No
- Change the data type of a field
- Add a new field
- Reorder fields
- Use Access online help

New words

At the end of this chapter you should be able to explain the following term:
- Data type

Changing and deleting database records

I n Chapter 2 you discovered how to create a single-table database in Access. Now it's time to learn how to modify your table in various ways. To change or delete a record in your Birds database, open Access, open the Birds database, and then open the Birds table. By default, your table opens in Datasheet view.

Changing a field

To change data in a field, begin by clicking on that field.

- If you click on the extreme left of the field, the entire field is selected and anything you type immediately overwrites the whole field.

- If you click anywhere else in the field, you can use the Backspace or Delete key to delete characters one by one, or you can insert new characters.

Remember that you cannot change the Number field – it is assigned by Access. Change the Migratory? checkbox by clicking it. If it is already on, clicking it turns it off; if it is off, clicking it turns it on. (If the Migratory? field contains 'No', you can either leave it alone or change it to 'Yes'; no other input is accepted.)

Deleting a record

To delete a record, select it by clicking anywhere in it: Access shows an arrowhead at the extreme left. Then choose **Edit | Delete Record**, or click the Delete Record button on the toolbar. You can then confirm that you want to delete the record, or change your mind and leave it alone.

Indicates a selected record

Delete Record button

Exercise 3.1: Changing and deleting data

1   Open Access, select the Open an existing file option, select your Birds database, and click **OK**.

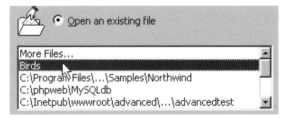

Display your Birds table in Datasheet view.

2   Change two fields containing incorrect information in record 20 for the Pheasant.

The Colour should be Red/Black. The Size should be 53.

3   Delete record 21, concerning the Dodo. It is once more extinct!

4   Type the details shown in the Date Seen and Place Seen fields.

Notice that the Date Seen field accepts only valid dates, and forces you to input them in a standard way.

Number	Date Seen	Place Seen
1		
2	13/09/99	Dalkey
3	04/09/98	Stephen's Green
4	12/06/98	Ireland's Eye
5		
6		
7		
8		
9	12/06/98	Ireland's Eye
10		
11	14/06/99	Malahide
12	12/12/98	Dollymount
13		
14		
15		
16	28/09/98	Wexford
17	28/09/98	Wexford
18		
19		
20	08/08/81	Wexford
22	07/06/99	Ballsbridge

5 When you are finished, close the table.

You are then returned to the Database window.

If your database records contain an AutoNumber field, and you delete a record, Access does *not* reassign the number of the deleted record to another record. Access ensures that records keep the number initially assigned to them, and it always assigns higher numbers to later additions than to earlier ones.

The different data types

At this stage, if you've followed the exercises, you're probably thinking that Access is reading your mind. How does it know that the Date Seen column should only contain dates? And how does it know that the Migratory? column is either ticked for Yes, or left blank for No? (Or that input in that field is limited to Yes and No.) Well, the answer is in the table design, and, to be honest, we cheated a bit.

When you set up a table in Access, there are two things you have to do for each field:

- You have to give the field a *name*, and

- You have to give the field a *data type*.

When you used the Wizard to set up the Birds table, the fields you selected from the Plants sample table had the same characteristics as the corresponding fields in the Birds table. You changed the names of the fields to match the bird-watching application. However, because you chose fields carefully, you didn't have to change the data types.

The data type tells Access how to treat the field, how the data is to be stored, and what kind of data is allowed in it.

Data type

This determines the kind of data that you can store in a field, and tells Access how to handle it.

Access recognizes a number of different data types. The most important ones for our purposes are shown as follows:

Data Type	Used For	Examples
Text	Any sort of alphabetic or numeric data. Typically used where there is a limit on the amount of data. No more than 255 characters may be input. (If the data is numeric, it cannot be used in calculations.)	Surname, Colour, Postal Code, Telephone Number
Memo	Any sort of alphabetic or numeric data. Typically used for free-form input. Up to	Description, Where Seen, Notes

	64,000 characters may be input. (Again, if the data is numeric, it cannot be used in calculations.)	
Number	Numeric data that may be used in calculations.	Quantity in Stock, Number in Flock, Number Sold
Date/Time	Date or time data.	Date Bought, Arrival Time, Planting Date
Currency	Money values or other numeric data used in calculations where the number of decimal places does not exceed four.	Price, Current Value
AutoNumber	A number assigned to each new record automatically. Access assigns the numbers in sequence, starting with 1.	Sequence Number
Yes/No	Fields that can have simple yes/no, true/false, or on/off values only.	Migratory?, Buy Again?, Flowering?

Changing data types

It is easy to change the data type of a field, but ideally you should get it right at the design stage. If you try to change the data type after you have input a lot of data, you can confuse Access, and you may lose some of your data.

In Exercise 3.2 you will change some of the data types in the Birds table.

Exercise 3.2: Changing data types

1 Display your Birds table in Design view. You can see that the window is divided into two main panes.

```
Birds : Table
      Field Name          Data Type
🔑▶ Number              AutoNumber
    Bird Name            Text
    Colour               Text
    Migratory?           Yes/No
    Size                 Text
    Date Seen            Date/Time
    Place Seen           Text
```

At the top is the list of field names with their data types.

2 Click on any of the Data Type fields. A drop-down arrow appears beside the data type. Click on this arrow: you see the list of data types described above (along with a few others that we haven't discussed). To change a data type, you simply select the new one from that list.

```
Birds : Table
      Field Name          Data Type
🔑 Number              AutoNumber
▶  Bird Name            Text            ▼
   Colour               Text
   Migratory?           Memo
   Size                 Number
   Date Seen            Date/Time
   Place Seen           Currency
                        AutoNumber
                        Yes/No
                        OLE Object
                        Hyperlink
                        Lookup Wizard...
```

3 Try some experiments.

- Change the Data Type of Migratory? from Yes/No to Number. Close the table, and confirm that you want to save the changes. Then open the table in Datasheet view. Notice how the data displayed under Migratory? has changed.

- Go back into Design view. (To do this, click the Design view button in the toolbar, or close the table and then click the Design button again.) This time, change the data type of Migratory? to Date/Time.

Then save the change and have a look at the effect of this change on the data displayed in the datasheet. Notice how changing the data type after you have input data can yield surprising results.

When you have finished experimenting, change the data type of Migratory? back to Yes/No.

A check box

4 If the Migratory? field contains 'Yes' or 'No', change it to a checkbox, as follows.

- Click on the Migratory? field.

- Then, in the lower pane (Field Properties), click the Lookup tab, and, in Display Control, select the option you want: checkbox.

General	Lookup	
Display Control	Check Box	▾

5 In later exercises you will want to compare the sizes of different birds. To do this, the Size field must be numeric. So change its data type from Text to Number.

6 Finally, close the table and, when prompted, save your changes.

Adding new fields to your table

Can you add new fields to your database records at any time? Yes. As you will discover in Exercise 3.3, you can add new fields in either Design or Datasheet view.

A danger of adding new fields is that you may have to go back and edit all records you have already entered. This applies particularly to numeric fields (where a blank field may be interpreted as 0), and Yes/No fields (where a blank field may be interpreted as No), but it is also important for any field that you use for sorting or filtering data.

So it is better if you think about the fields you want when you are setting up the database, and modify the design as little as possible after that.

Exercise 3.3: Adding new fields

1 Display your Birds table in Design view.

2 Where do you want to add a new field: at the end of a record or somewhere in the middle?

   • To add the new field between two existing fields, click on the title of the field that will be on the right of the new field and choose **Insert | Field**.

   • To add a new field at the end of the record, click on the next unused Field Name box. For this exercise, select this option.

3 Enter the title of the new field: Comments.

4 Specify the data type of the new field: Memo.

Size	Number
Date Seen	Date/Time
Place Seen	Text
▶ Comments	Text
	Text
	Memo
	Number
	Date/Time
	Currency
	AutoNumber

(A field with Text data type may hold a maximum of 255 characters, whereas a field with Memo data type may hold up to 64,000 characters.)

5 Switch to Datasheet view. You will be asked to save your table: click **Yes**.

6 Click on the heading of the Migratory? column and choose **Insert | Column**.

(When you insert a new column, Access always positions the new column to the left of the currently selected column.)

7 By default, Access assigns a data type of Text to a new column. If that is what you want, fine.

In this exercise, it isn't. Switch to Design view, and change the data type to Number. Also, type a field name of 'Number Seen'.

Number	Number Seen
1	23
2	21
3	14
4	5
5	3
6	7
7	17
8	1
9	3
10	4
11	12
12	34
13	22
14	16
15	9
16	14
17	16
18	1
19	2
20	6
22	4

Colour	Text
▶ Number Seen	Number
Migratory?	Yes/No

8 Switch to Datasheet view, saving the table as you do. Enter the numbers as shown on the left.

When finished, save your table.

Reordering the fields in a table

To change the order of fields in the table, click on the title of the one you want to move. Then click on it again, but this time maintain the click (keep pressure on the left button): note that a box appears on the tail of the cursor.

Cursor shape for reordering fields

Now drag it to the new location to the left or right. When you arrive at your chosen destination, notice how a bold line has appeared, indicating Access's understanding of where you want to place your moving column: if this is correct, release your finger from the mouse button, and the column moves.

Colour	Number Seen	Migratory?
hite	23	Yes

Try this a number of times until you are confident about it.

Saving to a diskette

Have you been saving your table as you went along?
You should, using either the **File | Save** command or
the Save button on the toolbar.

Save button

Once a database has been saved, Access does
not normally thereafter prompt you to save changes when
you exit – it assumes, unlike most Microsoft applications, that
any changes you make are changes you want to keep.

It is also a good idea to save a copy of your database on a
diskette. Exercise 3.4 follows the method recommended by
Microsoft's website for copying an Access 2000 database.

Exercise 3.4: Saving your Access database to a diskette

1 Insert a diskette in the diskette drive of your computer:

   • If it is a new diskette, ensure that it is formatted.

   • If it is a previously used one, ensure that there is
     sufficient space on it to hold your Birds database. (It
     should be about 220KB.)

2 Close the Birds table, and close the database that
   contains it by closing the Database window.

3 Open Windows Explorer. In the left-hand pane, click on
   the drive that contains your Birds database. The folder
   contents of the drive appear in the right-hand pane.

4 In the right-hand pane, double-click the folder that
   contains the database file. For example, the My
   Documents folder.

5 Click the Birds database file once to select it, and choose **Edit | Copy**.

6 In the left-hand pane, click on the A: drive, and choose **Edit | Paste**.

You have successfully saved a copy of Birds on the floppy diskette.

Online help

Like Excel, PowerPoint and other Microsoft applications, Access offers a searchable online help system. The word 'help' means that the information is there to assist you understand and use the application. The word 'online' means that the material is presented on the computer screen rather than as a traditional printed manual.

You can search through and read online help in two ways: from the **Help** menu, or from dialog boxes.

Using Help menu options

Choose **Help | Contents and Index** to display the following three tabs of the Help Topics dialog box.

Contents tab

This offers short descriptions of Access's main features.

Where you see a heading with a book symbol, double-click it to view the related sub-headings.

Double-click on a question mark symbol to read the help text. Click a double-arrow to view step-by-step instructions.

Answer Wizard

Type your question in the box at the top-left of the dialog box, and click Search. Access displays a list of suggested help topics in the lower-left. Click on a topic to display the associated text in the right pane.

Index tab

Type the word or phrase you are interested in and click Search. Access displays all matches from the online help in the lower-left of the dialog box. When you find the index entry that you are looking for, click on it to display the associated text in the right pane.

As you search through and read online help topics, you will see the following buttons at the top of the online help window:

- **Hide/Show**: Hides or displays the left pane of the online help dialog box.

- **Back/Forward**: Moves you backwards and forwards through previously visited help topics.

- **Print**: Prints the currently displayed help topic.

- **Options**: Offers a number of display choices.

Take a few minutes to look through Access's online help system. Remember that you will be free to use online help during an ECDL test.

Using help from the screen

You can also access online help directly from any Access screen, as Exercise 3.5 demonstrates.

Exercise 3.5: Using online help from an Access screen

1 Display your Birds table in Datasheet view, and choose **Format | Datasheet**.

2 Click the question-mark symbol near the top right of the dialog box. Access displays a question mark to the right of the cursor.

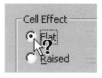

3 Drag the mouse down and right, and click on the Flat option.

4 Access displays online help text telling you about the purpose of the selected screen element.

> Select a cell effect for the datasheet. The sunken and raised cell effects default to a silver background color.

5 Click anywhere else on the Access screen to remove the online help text, and click **Cancel** to close the dialog box.

Practise this exercise with other dialog boxes in Access.

When finished, you can close your table and database, and quit Access.

Access toolbars

The most frequently used Access functions are available by clicking a single button on the toolbar.

Normally, Access displays the most suitable toolbar – the one containing the buttons for the functions that you are most likely to use.

If you want to hide the toolbar (and choose all your options from the menus), or if you want to display other toolbars, choose **View | Toolbar** and select the toolbars that you want displayed.

Chapter summary: so now you know

A field's *data type* tells Access how to treat the field, how the data is to be stored, and what kind of data is allowed in it. Commonly used data types are: Text, Memo, Number, Date/Time, Currency, AutoNumber and Yes/No.

Try to select the correct data type for each field before you enter data, because changing a field's data type at a later stage may result in data loss.

You can add new fields to the database at any time, but you may need to go back and edit all records that you have already entered, particularly for numeric fields (where a blank field may be interpreted as 0), and Yes/No fields (where a blank may be interpreted as No).

Access offers a searchable *online help* system that you can access in two ways: from the Help menu, and from the question-mark button at the top-right of individual dialog boxes.

CHAPTER 4

Making the database work for you

In this chapter

After Chapters 2 and 3 you might still be asking: why bother? You can use a word processor to keep lists of things, and if you want to put them in neat columns, you can use a spreadsheet. Well, this chapter should convince you that a database is a very useful tool for managing your information, and for quickly finding the particular items of interest.

For example, the order in which you entered records originally in your table may not be the order in which, later on, you would prefer to display those records. You could reorder – *sort* – a table of customers, for instance, so that the biggest spenders appear at the top of the list. You can even save sorts you use regularly as *queries* so that you can apply them at the click of a button.

Another very useful feature is *filtering* – the ability to reduce the amount of information displayed, either by showing fewer fields in each record, or by showing only those records that satisfy certain criteria.

Finally, as with other Microsoft Office applications, Access includes a *Find* feature that enables you to locate a particular item quickly.

New skills

At the end of this section you should be able to:
- Reorder (sort) the database records
- Save a sort as a query and apply it to a database
- Find a particular record or set of records
- Use the Access Find feature

New words

At the end of this section you should be able to explain the following terms:
- Sort
- Sort order
- Find
- Filter
- Query

Changing the order of records in the table

Open Access and open your Birds table. Notice that the datasheet shows the records in the order you entered them: the Number field reflects that order – records you added later have higher numbers than ones you added earlier.

However, you can choose to display the records in a different order, by *sorting* them.

Sort

An operation that you carry out on a table to change the order in which the records are displayed. Sorting does not change the content of records, only their location.

Access offers two sequencing options, called sort orders.

Sort order

A particular way of ordering records based on field values. A sort order can be in alphabetic ascending (A to Z) or descending (Z to A) sequence.

Sort Ascending button

Suppose you want the records to be displayed alphabetically by bird name, or in order of size (biggest first, smallest last), how would you go

about it? Easy. Click on any Bird Name field. Then
click the Sort Ascending button on the toolbar. Done!

Click on any Size field. Click the Sort   *Sort Descending*
Descending button. Again, done! What could   *button*
be simpler?

Number	Bird Name
22	Blue Tit
12	Brent Goose
9	Cormorant
5	Fulmar
4	Gannet
15	Goldeneye
2	Great Crested Grebe
1	Great Northern Diver
6	Great Shearwater
10	Grey Heron
13	Greylag Goose
19	Kestrel
3	Little Grebe
17	Mallard
7	Manx Shearwater
11	Mute Swan
20	Pheasant
14	Shelduck
18	Sparrowhawk
8	Storm Petrel
16	Teal

Number	Bird Name	Size
11	Mute Swan	114
10	Grey Heron	90
4	Gannet	85
9	Cormorant	83
13	Greylag Goose	76
1	Great Northern Diver	69
14	Shelduck	57
12	Brent Goose	56
17	Mallard	55
20	Pheasant	53
2	Great Crested Grebe	46
5	Fulmar	45
6	Great Shearwater	42
15	Goldeneye	41
16	Teal	34
19	Kestrel	33
7	Manx Shearwater	30
18	Sparrowhawk	28
3	Little Grebe	24
8	Storm Petrel	13
22	Blue Tit	6

Sorted by name, ascending   *Sorted by size, descending*

These kinds of sorts are called simple, or *single criterion sorts*.
Now imagine that you have more complex requirements: you
want to sort all the birds by colour, and you want to show the
biggest birds of any colour before the smaller ones. These are
called *multiple criteria sorts*: you cannot use the sort buttons to
perform them. Exercise 4.1 shows you how to do them.

Exercise 4.1: Sorting records using a number of criteria

1 Open the Birds table in Datasheet view. Choose **Records
   | Filter | Advanced Filter/Sort**.

2 In the lower pane of the dialog box, click the list arrow button in the first row, first column. Access shows a list of all the fields in your table. Select Colour.

Field:	Size
Sort:	Bird Name
Criteria:	Colour
or:	Number Seen
	Migratory?
	Size
	Date Seen
	Place Seen
	Comments

3 Click in the second field in the first column. Access displays a list button at the right of the field. Click on this to select a sort order. Select Ascending.

4 Click in the first field of the second column: a list button is displayed. Click on it, and select Size from the list.

5 Click in the field below Size: a list button is displayed. Click on it and select Descending.

Field:	Colour	Size
Sort:	Ascending	Descending
Criteria:		
or:		

6 Click the Apply Filter button in the toolbar, and the datasheet is shown, this time listing the birds in order of colour, and with the bigger birds of each colour shown before the smaller ones.

Apply Filter button

Number	Bird Name	Colour	Number Seen	Migratory?	Size
3	Little Grebe	Black/Brown	14	☐	24
9	Cormorant	Black/White	3	☐	83
1	Great Northern Diver	Black/White	23	☑	69
12	Brent Goose	Black/White	34	☑	56
7	Manx Shearwater	Black/White	17	☐	30
8	Storm Petrel	Black/White	1	☐	13
18	Sparrowhawk	Blue/White	1	☑	28
22	Blue Tit	Blue/Yellow/Black/White	4	☐	6
17	Mallard	Green/White/Brown	16	☐	55
13	Greylag Goose	Grey	22	☑	76
19	Kestrel	Grey/Brown	2	☐	33
16	Teal	Grey/Multicolour	14	☐	34
10	Grey Heron	Grey/White	4	☐	90
2	Great Crested Grebe	Grey/White/Brown	21	☐	46
20	Pheasant	Red/Black	6	☐	53
11	Mute Swan	White	12	☐	114
4	Gannet	White/Black	5	☐	85
15	Goldeneye	White/Black	9	☑	41
6	Great Shearwater	White/Brown	7	☑	42
14	Shelduck	White/Brown/Black	16	☐	57
5	Fulmar	White/Grey	3	☐	45

7   Close your table, saving it as you do.

Why is the button called Apply Filter? Well, Access regards this kind of sort as a particular example of a filter. What's a filter? Don't worry about that for now: we'll be looking at filters a little later.

Saving a query

If you experiment with sorting, you'll see that you can view the information in your table in many different ways. You can, for example, separate the records into migratory and non-migratory birds; you can quickly identify the smallest bird you saw on a particular date; or you can list the birds you have seen in Wexford.

It's quite likely that you will want to repeat some of these sorts regularly. For example, if you have several hundred birds in your database, sorting them by colour and size would help you identify unusual birds. You can enter the sort criteria each time you want to sort the table in this way, or you can make life easy for yourself, by saving the sort criteria as a query.

Query
> *Queries are used to repeatedly view database records in a particular way defined by you.*

Exercise 4.2 shows you how to save your sort criteria as a query.

Exercise 4.2: Saving sort criteria as a query

1   Display your Birds table in Datasheet view. The sort criteria that you applied in Exercise 4.1 should still control the order in which the fields are listed.

2 Choose **Records | Filter | Advanced Filter/Sort**
to display the Filter dialog box. Choose **File |**
Save As Query or click the Save As Query
button on the toolbar.

Save As
Query button

3 Give the query a name: say Colour/Size.

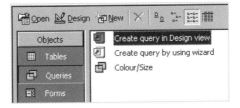

4 Click **OK**, and close the Filter dialog box. Close your
table. Access displays the Database window.

And that's it! Notice that the query shows up on the Queries
section of the Database window. From now on, even after you
have added more records to the database, or changed the
ones that are already there, you simply open this query and
the records in the table will be presented in the manner
defined by the query.

Note that queries don't make any permanent change to the
database; they simply extract information and present it in a
certain way.

If you have used a query to view a table in a particular
order, you can return to an unsorted view by choosing
Records | Remove Filter/Sort.

Notice that in this query all of the fields were shown. What
if we want to view only selected columns?

Exercise 4.3: Creating a query for selected columns only

1 On the Database window, click the Queries icon; then click the New button on that toolbar.

2 Select Design View and click **OK**.

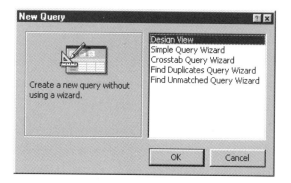

3 In the Tables tab select the Birds table. Click the **Add** button, followed by the **Close** button.

4 Now, as in Exercise 4.1, select Colour in the first Field column and choose Sort Ascending; then select Size in the second Field column, and choose Sort Descending.

5 Select Bird Name in the third Field column, but this time don't specify a Sort order.

Field:	Colour	Size	Bird Name ▾
Table:	Birds	Birds	Birds
Sort:	Ascending	Descending	
Show:	☑	☑	☑
Criteria:			
or:			

6 Click the **Run** button on the toolbar.

This time your Query returns only the referenced columns, and cuts out unnecessary or unwanted information in adjacent columns.

Run button

Colour	Size	Bird Name
▶ Black/Brown	24	Little Grebe
Black/White	83	Cormorant
Black/White	69	Great Northern Diver
Black/White	56	Brent Goose
Black/White	30	Manx Shearwater
Black/White	13	Storm Petrel
Blue/White	28	Sparrowhawk
Blue/Yellow/Black/White	6	Blue Tit
Green/White/Brown	55	Mallard
Grey	76	Greylag Goose
Grey/Brown	33	Kestrel
Grey/Multicolour	34	Teal
Grey/White	90	Grey Heron
Grey/White/Brown	46	Great Crested Grebe
Red/Black	53	Pheasant
White	114	Mute Swan
White/Black	85	Gannet
White/Black	41	Goldeneye
White/Brown	42	Great Shearwater
White/Brown/Black	57	Shelduck
White/Grey	45	Fulmar
*	0	

7 Close the dialog box. You are prompted to save the query – click the **Yes** button. Give the query a name you will remember, such as '3-Column, Colour/Size/Bird Name'. Click **OK**, and it's saved. You can subsequently view the selected fields of the table in the order you specified, simply by opening the query from the Queries section of the Database window.

Restricting the information displayed

You can reduce the amount of information displayed, either by showing fewer fields in each record, or by showing only those records that satisfy certain criteria. This is called filtering.

Filter

A filter restricts the display of your database information to records and fields that satisfy criteria that you specify.

Suppose, for example, you want to concentrate on birds that you have seen in Wexford. Simply find any record that matches your criterion – in this case, one with Wexford in the Place Seen column.

Click on the relevant field – Wexford – and then click on the Filter by Selection button in the toolbar.

Filter by Selection button

The display is immediately restricted to records that match your selection – that is, ones that have Wexford in the Place Seen column.

Number	Bird Name	Colour	Number Seen	Migratory?	Size	Date Seen	Place Seen
17	Mallard	Green/White/Brown	16	☐	55	28/09/98	Wexford
19	Kestrel	Grey/Brown	2	☐	33	27/09/98	Wexford
16	Teal	Grey/Multicolour	14	☐	34	28/09/98	Wexford

Don't panic: the rest of your records are still in the database. The filter just limits the amount of information in the display. To see all your records again, you remove the filter: click the Remove Filter button in the toolbar.

Remove Filter button

A word of caution: Recall that you can change the information in the database at any time. And recall that you change a Yes/No checkbox field by clicking on it: a click turns it on if it was off, and off if it was on. If you are filtering based on a Yes/No checkbox field, you will change the information when you select it. So in the case of a Yes/No checkbox field, you will have to click on the field twice before you click on the Filter by Selection button.

For example, suppose you want to study migratory birds only. As before, find one record of a migratory bird. Click on the Migratory? checkbox: notice what happens – the box changes from checked (Yes, migratory) to unchecked (No, not migratory). Click it again, so that it shows the correct status, and then click the Filter by Selection button. The display shows only migratory birds. Click the Remove Filter button.

Colour	Number Seen	Migratory?	Size	Date Seen	Place Seen
Black/White	23	☑	69		
Black/White	34	☑	56	12/12/98	Dollymount
Blue/White	1	☑	28		
Grey	22	☑	76		
White/Black	9	☑	41		
White/Brown	7	☑	42		
	0	☐	0		

Filtering by selection

When you select a field, and then filter based on the contents of that field, the process is known as *filtering by selection*. Note that you don't have to select the whole field: you might be interested in all the warblers, or all birds that have the colour grey somewhere. No problem.

Selecting part of a field for filtering by selection

As before, find a record that has the characteristic you want – say grey as one of its colours. Click and drag the mouse over the part of the field that has the word (or part of the word) that you want to match – in this case grey.

Then click the Filter by Selection button. The display shows the birds that have grey at the start of their colour field.

Number	Bird Name	Colour	Number Seen	Migratory?
2	Great Crested Grebe	Grey/White/Brown	21	☐
10	Grey Heron	Grey/White	4	☐
13	Greylag Goose	Grey	22	☑
16	Teal	Grey/Multicolour	14	☐
19	Kestrel	Grey/Brown	2	☐

A word of caution: Filtering by selection includes the ideas 'Beginning with ...' and 'Ending with ...'. If you select the first letter in a field and filter by selection, Access displays all records in which the field *begins with* that letter. Similarly, if you select the last letter in the field, Access displays the records in which the field *ends with* that letter.

So if you want to filter based on the first word or the last word in a field, include the first letter or the last letter only if you want to restrict the display to records that begin with or end with the selection. If you want all records that include the word anywhere in the field, select only *part* of the word – a part in the middle of the word, such as 'hit' for white or 'lac' for black.

Try filtering by selection yourself: remove the colour filter, and this time restrict the display to grebes.

Filtering filtered records

If you want to further restrict the records displayed – say to all green-coloured birds spotted in Wexford – you simply repeat the steps above. First, find all the birds spotted in Wexford, then from that list find all the green birds. Alternatively, start by finding all the green birds, and then further restrict that list to ones spotted in Wexford.

When finished, remove the filter.

Creating queries that filter records

In the next two Exercises, you will create and edit a query that filters records.

Exercise 4.4: Saving filters as a query

1 Display the Birds table in Datasheet view.

2 In the Colour column, select the word Grey in any field, then click the Filter by Selection button.

3 In the Place Seen column, select a field that contains the word Wexford and click the Filter by Selection button again.

4 Sort the records into ascending order by Bird Name.

5 Choose **Records | Filter | Advanced Filter/Sort** to display the Filter dialog box. Choose **File | Save As Query**, or click the Save as Query button on the toolbar.

6 Give the query a name: say Filtered records.

7 Click **OK**, and close the Filter dialog box. Close your table.

To see what the Filtered records query looks like, open it in the Queries section of the Database window and switch to Design view.

Field:	Bird Name	Colour	Place Seen
Table:	Birds	Birds	Birds
Sort:	Ascending		
Show:	☐	☐	☐
Criteria:		Like "grey*"	"wexford"
or:			

This query sorts the entries in the Bird Name into ascending order, and filters for records containing Grey in the Colour field and Wexford in the Place Seen field.

The criteria for Colour and Place Seen are on one line, and so are combined using logical AND: a record will be displayed only if it satisfies both criteria. If the criteria were on different lines, they would be combined using logical OR: a record will be displayed if it satisfies any of the criteria.

Exercise 4.5: Adding and removing fields in a query

1   Open the Filtered records query in the Queries section of the Database window, and switch to Design view.

2   Select the Place Seen field and choose **Edit | Delete Columns** to remove the field from the query.

3   Click in the empty field beside the Colour field, then click the arrow that appears at the right of the field to see a drop-down list of the fields in the Birds table. Select Number Seen.

4   In the second criteria row for the Number Seen field, enter >10.

5   Switch to the datasheet view of your query. The records shown are sorted by Bird Name in ascending order, and are filtered to include any record where either Grey appears in the Colour field OR more than 10 birds were seen.

6   Save your query, then close it.

Find

Is there a quick way of finding a particular record among hundreds or thousands? Yes. Use the Access Find feature. You can run Find in any of the following ways: choose **Edit | Find**, click the Find button on the toolbar, or use the keyboard shortcut Ctrl+f.

Find button

Try the following exercise to find a specific record in the Birds table.

Exercise 4.6: Finding a specific record

1 Display the Birds table in Datasheet view. Click the Find button on the toolbar.

2 In the Find What field, type the following:

Goldeneye

In the Look In: box, select Birds: Table. In Match:, select Whole Field.

3 Click the **Find Next** button and Access should highlight the Goldeneye record.

4 Click the **Find Next** button. Access indicates that there are no further records that satisfy the criterion. Click **OK**.

5 In the Find dialog box, click the **Close** button.

6 Now, on your own, and in separate Find operations, find the following data:

- **Malahide** – This should highlight the Mute Swan record.

- **55** – This should highlight the Mallard record.

- **Grey** – This should highlight the Greylag Goose record – this is the only record for which 'grey' is a whole field.

Now change the Match field to read 'Any Part of Field', and find grey again. This time when you click the **Find Next** button repeatedly, a number of other records should be highlighted – these are records that have 'grey' somewhere in the field.

Well done. You have completed Chapter 4. You can close your Birds table and close Access.

Chapter summary: so now you know

A *sort* is an operation that you carry out on a table to change the order in which the records are displayed. Access allows you to perform single criterion and multiple criteria sort operations.

If you perform a particular sort regularly, you can save the sort details as a *query*. You can use queries to view repeatedly database records in a particular way defined by you.

Filtering is the process of reducing the amount of information displayed by Access, either by showing fewer fields in each record, or by showing only those records that satisfy certain criteria. To view all your records again, remove the filter.

You can filter a table by clicking on a particular field, or by dragging the mouse over the word (or part of a word) that you want to match, and then clicking on the Filter by Selection button on the toolbar.

Note that if you are filtering based on a Yes/No field, you need to click on the field twice before you click on the Filter by Selection button. A single click on a Yes/No field will change the information in that field!

You can filter the result of a filter operation to restrict further the information displayed.

Access's *Find* feature provides a quick way of locating a particular record or records based on their field values.

CHAPTER 5

Working with forms

In this chapter

Until now, you have been looking at your database records
in Datasheet view – they have been shown in rows, with a
column for each field. Datasheet view can make reading the
information difficult, and it's annoying if the fields and
records extend beyond the edges of your screen, so that
you have to scroll left and right and up and down to see the
items of interest.

Forms are better for those times when all you really want
is to see information relating to a single record at one time,
laid out in an attractive manner. Forms have the added
advantage of being much easier to read, and you can
design different, eye-pleasing forms for different purposes.

As you will learn in this chapter, everything you can do in a datasheet you can also do in a form. You can input new records and change existing records; you can sort the records into a different order; and you can filter the records so that only ones that satisfy your criteria are displayed.

New skills

At the end of this chapter you should be able to:
- Create a form to display records, in whole or in part, one at a time
- Use a form to create new records
- Use a form to search for and modify a record
- Modify a form that you have previously created
- Import an image or graphic file into a form

New words

You can relax: there are no new words in this chapter.

Forms: what are they for?

R emember in Chapter 1 you learnt that Access enables you to view and manipulate information in two ways:

- **Datasheet view**: This shows the information for many records, arranged in columns and rows.

- **Form view**: This presents information for one record at a time.

Creating your form with the Form Wizard

Forms are based on tables. You can create a form only *after* you have created a table, such as the Birds table created in Chapter 2. In Exercise 5.1 you will use the Access Form Wizard to create a new form.

Exercise 5.1: Creating a form

1   Open Access, open your Birds database, and click the Forms icon.

Click the New button on the toolbar. As
with the Table Wizard, the Form Wizard
offers a number of semi-automated options.

New button

2 Select, for example, the AutoForm:
Columnar option, select the Birds table, and have a look
at the result.

When finished, click the Close button to close the form
– but don't save it.

3 Starting again from the Forms
section of the Database window,
click the New button. This time,
choose the Form Wizard.

> Design View
> Form Wizard
> AutoForm: Columnar
> AutoForm: Tabular
> AutoForm: Datasheet
> Chart Wizard
> PivotTable Wizard

> Birds

4 Select the table on which the
form is based – Birds.

5 Click **OK**. This starts the
Form Wizard.

6 You've seen something like this before, when you used
the Table Wizard to design your Birds table in Chapter 2.
The screen shows two list boxes:

• On the left you can see all the fields in the table.

• On the right you can see the fields that you have chosen
to include in the form. Initially, the right list is empty.

Move the fields you want to use in your form from the
Available Fields box to the Selected Fields box by using
the arrow buttons.

For this exercise, move the fields shown. When finished,
click the **Next** button.

Tables/Queries

Table: Birds

Available Fields:

Number
Colour
Number Seen
Migratory?
Size
Comments

Selected Fields:

Bird Name
Date Seen
Place Seen

7 The Form Wizard then presents
   you with four possible layouts for
   the form. You can get an idea of
   what each is like by selecting
   them in turn. The best for your
   purposes is Columnar. Select this
   one, and click the **Next** button.

   ○ Columnar
   ○ Tabular
   ○ Datasheet
   ○ Justified

8 The Form Wizard then offers you a choice of styles for
   the form. Again, you can preview styles by selecting
   them in turn.

   Select Standard and click the **Next** button.

   Blends
   Blueprint
   Expedition
   Industrial
   International
   Ricepaper
   SandStone
   Standard
   Stone
   Sumi Painting

   xxx
   xxx
   xxxx

   Label Data

9 Access suggests a name for the form: change this to 'Birds Spotted' to make it easier to identify later.

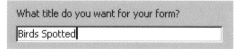

You can then either use the form immediately, or go back and modify it. Select the option to Open the form, and click the **Finish** button.

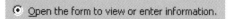

You can then use the form to view selected information from the records in your table.

Using your form to view records

When you finish Exercise 5.1 you are immediately presented with a Form view of the Birds table. The form shows the selected fields from the first record in the table.

Bird Name	Great Northern Diver
Date Seen	
Place Seen	

Click the Close box to close the form.

At other times, to get to the same point, you start from the Database window, click the Form icon, and double-click Birds Spotted form.

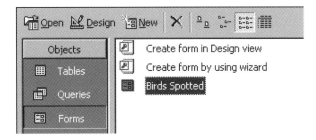

Navigating in Form view

You can step through the different records one at a time by using the navigation buttons shown along the bottom of the form.

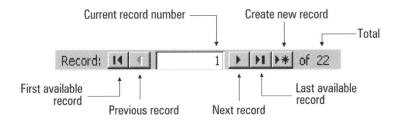

Sorting in Form view

As in Datasheet view, you can sort the records by selection: click on the field that you want to use as the basis for the sort, and click the Sort Ascending or Sort Descending button in the toolbar.

You can also perform a multiple-criteria sort, in exactly the same way as in Datasheet view: choose **Records | Filter | Advanced Filter/Sort.**

Filtering by selection in Form view

In Form view, you can filter records by selection, exactly as you did in Datasheet view: find a record that meets your criterion, select the relevant field (or the part of it that is of interest) and click the Filter by Selection button in the

*Filter by
Selection button*

toolbar. You will see that the number of records shown beside the navigation buttons reflects the smaller number of records that satisfies your criterion.

As in Datasheet view, you can filter these records again to refine further the search for the records that you are interested in.

Filtering by Form

Another option is to Filter by Form. For example, in Exercise 5.2 you will learn how to restrict the records displayed to those of birds that you have actually spotted.

Exercise 5.2: Using a form to filter records

1   Open the Birds Spotted form. Click the Filter by Form button in the toolbar or choose **Records | Filter | Filter by Form**.

*Filter by Form
button*

Access displays a form, into which you can enter your filter criteria. In this case, the date is the criterion of interest.

2   Click on the Date Seen field. Notice the arrow that appears to the right of the field. Click the arrow to view a drop-down list that shows all the dates on which you

recorded sightings. If you wanted to find all the birds you spotted on a specific date, you'd simply pick the date from the list.

3   What you want, however, is to find the birds you spotted on any date, that is, any record for which the date is not blank (or is greater than zero).

So enter the following in the Date Seen field: >0.

If Access has placed any values in the Bird Name or Place Seen fields, delete them.

4   Click the Apply Filter button in the toolbar: the first record with the date filled in is shown, and the record count shows the number of such records in the table.

⊞ **Birds Spotted**	_ □ ✕
▶ Bird Name	Great Crested Grebe
Date Seen	13/09/99
Place Seen	Dalkey
Record: ◄◄ ◄	1 ► ►I ►✱ of 10 (Filtered)

5   Click the Remove Filter button (as it is now) in the toolbar, and all the records in the table are again viewable.

Remove Filter button

Wildcards in filters and queries

You don't have to be precise when you are entering your filter criteria: you can use so-called *wildcards* to tell Access 'Give me everyone whose name includes Donnel', and it will get the Donnellys, McDonnells, MacDonnells, O'Donnells, and so on.

The most important wildcards are an asterisk (*) and a question mark (?). When you specify the criteria for a query or a filter, an asterisk (*) means 'anything or nothing', and a question mark (?) means 'any single character'.

Say, for example, you want to find all the birds that have 'Great' in their names. In the Bird Name field in the form, enter the following:

    Great

When you apply the filter, only the three records that include 'Great' will be displayed.

Or, if you want to find birds that are coloured black or brown, you construct a filter with the colour specified as b????. When you apply this filter, you will be presented only with records that have the colour specified as five characters beginning with the letter 'b'. You would not, for example, get blue birds (for the obvious reason that 'blue' has only four characters).

Creating an All Fields Form

The easiest way to enter information into your table is to use a form. However, if you are adding new records to the table, the form you created in Exercise 5.2 is not sufficiently detailed. You need a new form – one that enables you to fill in all the details for each bird (an 'All Fields Form'). Let's make one the quick way.

Exercise 5.3: Creating an all fields form

1 On the Database window, click the Forms icon. Click the New button.

2 Select AutoForm: Columnar, and specify the Birds table.

3 Click **OK**.

And that's it. Access now presents a new form, ready for use.

```
Design View
Form Wizard
AutoForm: Columnar
AutoForm: Tabular
AutoForm: Datasheet
Chart Wizard
PivotTable Wizard
```

```
Birds
```

```
Birds                                    _ □ ×
  Number            [        1]
  Bird Name         [Great Northern Diver]
  Colour            [Black/White]
  Number Seen       [        23]
  Migratory?        [✓]
  Size              [        69]
  Date Seen         [        ]
  Place Seen        [        ]
  Comments          [        ]

Record: ⏮ ◀ [        1] ▶ ⏭ ▶* of 21
```

4 Close your form, and save it with the name AllFields.

You can subsequently access this form at any time from the Forms section on the Database window, and use it to view the records in your table, to change them, or to create new records.

Using a form to create new records

To create new records, click the Create New Record button in the navigation bar at the bottom of the form. Access presents a new, blank form. Fill it in.

Create New Record button

You can complete the fields in any order by clicking in the field and entering the information. The easiest way to complete the form, however, is to fill in the first field (Access automatically positions the cursor there when you open the form), and then proceed in order through the fields either by pressing Tab or by pressing Enter. When you have filled in the last field in the form, press Tab or Enter to open up a new, blank form.

Exercise 5.4: Using a form to enter a new record

1   Open the AllFields form from the Database window. Click the Create New Record button and enter the details of the Golden Eagle as follows:

Bird Name:	Golden Eagle
Colour:	Golden Brown
Size:	120
Date Seen:	06/09/00
Place Seen:	Colorado

2   When finished, close the form.

To view the effect on your table, display your table in Datasheet view. Can't see the new record? Close your table and then open it again. Your new record is now visible.

Using a form to modify existing records

Any changes you make to the information in a form are reflected in the table. Remember that the Datasheet and the Form views are just two ways of looking at the same information.

To use the form to modify the information in your table, locate the record you are interested in (by paging through the records, one at a time, or by sorting or filtering), click on the field you want to change, and delete, overwrite, or add information.

Exercise 5.5: Using a form to modify records

1 Use the AllFields form to complete all the remaining empty fields in all the records in your table. Make up information – for the exercise, it doesn't have to be accurate, or even truthful!

2 When finished, close your AllFields form.

Modifying form layout and content

For the moment, and for most purposes, the Form Wizard does a fine job. However, Access enables you to design forms from scratch, and to redesign ones that have already been designed. For example, you can:

• Change the position, size and shape of fields

• Apply formatting to fields and field titles

• Insert a picture (such as a company logo) onto a form

You will explore the basics of these form design features (there is no need to go into this too deeply) in the following exercises.

Exercise 5.6: Creating a form in Design view

1   On the Database window, click the Form icon. Click the New button.

2   Select Design View, specify the Birds table, and click **OK**. Your screen should look as shown.

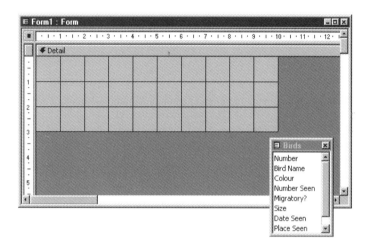

To add a new field to your form, you need the field list (that is, the list of fields in your table). If it is not already displayed, choose **View | Field List**.

3   Drag the following fields from the Field List to the form: Bird Name, Colour and Size.

(Hint: When releasing the mouse button, position the cursor in the centre rather than at the left of the form.) Your form should now look something like that shown.

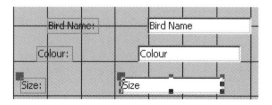

Notice how each field has a title and a textbox.

4 You need to 'tidy up' your form by repositioning the titles and textboxes. To change the position of a field:

- Click on the field textbox. A number of sizing handles are displayed around the textbox and the field title.

- Move the cursor anywhere over a border except on one of the handles. The cursor changes to an 'open hand' shape.

- Click and drag the field to its new location.

For small adjustments, display the 'open hand' as above, but rather than dragging with the mouse, hold down the Ctrl key and press an arrow key. Reposition your three field titles and textboxes until they look as shown below.

Bird Name:		Bird Name
Colour:		Colour
Size:		Size

5 By default, both the field title and textbox move together, and maintain their position relative to one another. To move the title or textbox independently, click in the textbox, and then click on the larger 'move handle' at the top-left of the box. The cursor changes to a 'pointing hand'.

You can then drag the field to its new location.

Reposition the titles and textboxes until your form looks as shown.

You might find this tricky to begin with, but it will become easier with practice.

6   Click the Form View button on the toolbar and admire your handiwork. Switch back to Design view by clicking the same button again.

Form View button

7   Close your form, saving it as Birds Colour/Size as you do.

You can change the size of the background area of a form in Design view by clicking on the boundary (the cursor changes to a double-headed arrow) and then dragging with the mouse.

In Exercises 5.7 and 5.8 you will change the appearance of your form. The Form toolbar, as you will discover, offers a wide range of formatting possibilities.

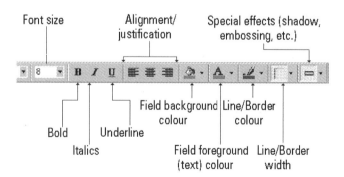

Remember, however, that the best forms are simple, are laid out clearly, and use colour and other graphics sparingly.

Exercise 5.7: Changing form layout in Design view

1 Open your Birds Colour/Size form in Design view.

(To do this, display the Database window, click the Forms icon; double-click the Birds Spotted form, and then click the Design View button.)

2 Click anywhere in the Bird Name title and click the Bold button on the toolbar. Repeat this action for the other two titles.

3 Click anywhere in the Bird Name textbox and click the Italic button on the toolbar. Repeat this action for the other two textboxes. Your fields should look as shown.

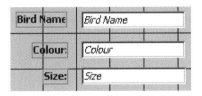

Feeling adventurous? Try changing the font or font colour of the field titles or textboxes.

4 Your next step is to change the size of the textboxes. To do this:

• Click a field to select it.

• Hold the cursor over a sizing handle. The cursor changes shape to a double-headed arrow.

• Drag the sizing handle in the required direction.

Increase the size of your three textboxes by dragging their right borders about two centimetres further to the right. Your fields should look like those shown.

5   Close your form, saving it as you do.

Want to add a picture to your form? Apply some colourful effects? Access makes it easy. Follow Exercise 5.8 to discover how.

Exercise 5.8: Inserting a picture into a form in Design view

1   Open your Birds Colour/Size form in Design view.

2   Choose **Insert | Picture**. Access displays a dialog box in which you specify the graphic you want to include in the form. You can navigate around the hard disk, diskette, or CD-ROM to find the picture you want. If you don't have one of your own, a variety is available in the following folder:

    C:\Program Files\Microsoft Office\Clipart\Popular

    Select the file named Dove in that sub-folder and then click **OK**. Access inserts the selected picture onto your form.

3   If the inserted picture is too large, right-click on it. From the pop-up menu displayed, choose **Properties**; then, on the Format tab, change Size Mode to Zoom.

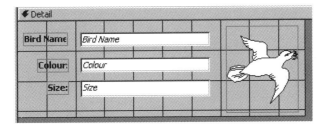

Close the dialog box; then click on one of the sizing handles at the corners of the picture, and drag it inwards to the required size.

To move the image to a different location on the form, click on the picture anywhere except on the sizing handles. Hold down the mouse button; the cursor changes to a hand. Now drag the picture to the right side of the form and release the mouse button.

Adjust the size of the background form area until your form looks as shown.

4 As a final step, let's add some colour to your form. Click the Bird Name textbox to select it, click the arrow to the right of the Fill Color button on the toolbar, and select the colour yellow. Repeat this action for the other two textboxes.

Fill Color button

5 Click anywhere on the form background, click the arrow to the right of the Fill Color button on the toolbar, and select the colour red.

6   Click the Form view button on the toolbar and admire your handiwork. Switch back to Design view by clicking the same button again.

7   Click the Close button to close your form, saving it as you do.

Well done. You have now completed Chapter 5. You may close your Birds database and close Access.

Chapter summary: so now you know

Forms enable you to view your database records one at a time. As forms are based on tables, you can create a form only *after* you have created a table. Both forms and the datasheet contain the *same information*: any change you make to data in a form is reflected immediately in the datasheet, and any change you make in a datasheet is reflected in the associated forms.

You can create forms quickly and easily with the Access *Form Wizard*. You simply select which fields from the table you want to include on your form, choose from a range of data layouts and decorative styles, and give your form a name.

You can use a form to view existing records in your database. A series of *navigation buttons* along the bottom of the form enable you to step through different records one at a time. Within Form view you can sort and filter records, and use *wildcard characters* (* and ?).

An *All Fields Form* is one that contains every field in your table, and is used typically for entering data. The fastest way to enter data is to fill in the first field and, pressing Tab or Enter after each one, proceed in order through the fields. When you have filled in the last field in the form, press Tab or Enter to open up a new, blank form.

To use a form to *modify* the information in your table, locate the record you are interested in (by paging through the records, one at a time, or by sorting or filtering), click on the field you want to change, and delete, overwrite, or add information. You can include graphic images in your forms.

In Design view you can change the formatting of both field titles and text boxes, adjust the shape and size of any field, add new fields, and import, resize and reposition graphic images.

CHAPTER 6

Working with reports

In this chapter

In the earlier chapters of this module you learnt how to put information into your database, and how to manipulate it and view it on-screen. In this chapter you will discover how to get information out, and how to present it in a useful and accessible way.

New skills

At the end of this chapter you should be able to:
- Present information you have extracted from the database on screen
- Print out a report of information from the database
- Create and customize headers and footers

New words

At the end of this chapter you should be able to explain the following terms:
- Report
- Grouped report

Your first report

Generally speaking, a report is a way of presenting information in printed form. However, the word is increasingly used to describe information in a form suitable for printing – even if it is only displayed on screen.

Report
> *A document (printed or on screen) that presents information in a structured way.*

You can, of course, print out any Access screen – such as the result of sorting or filtering records in Datasheet view. If these are adequate for your purposes, simply click the Print button on the toolbar, or choose **File | Print**.

Print button

However, Access's reporting options give you a great deal of control over how your information is presented. You can highlight important information, group data into categories, and give totals and count information for each category, subcategory, and for the entire report.

AutoReport

The simplest way to produce a report is to use the AutoReport feature. Its two options are:

- **AutoReport: Columnar.** Access prints each selected field on a separate line with the field name to its left.

- **AutoReport: Tabular.** Access prints the fields of each record on a single line. Field names are printed once at the top of each page of the report.

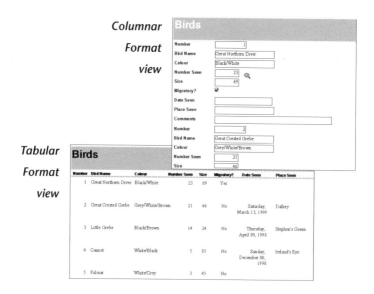

Columnar Format view

Tabular Format view

Let's begin by creating a report based on your Birds table.

Exercise 6.1: Producing a report with AutoReport

1   Open Access and open the Birds database. On the Database window, click the Reports icon, and click the New button on the toolbar.

New button

2 Select AutoReport: Columnar. In the drop-down list of tables and queries, specify the Birds table.

3 Click **OK** and admire the report on the screen. To view the various pages of your report, click the navigation buttons at the bottom left of your screen.

4 If you have a printer, click the Print button on the toolbar, or choose **File | Print**. Then hang your finished report on the wall.

5 Close the Report window, and (if it is displayed) close the Report Design window. You will be prompted to save. Name it 'My First Report' and click **Save**.

Report Wizard

While AutoReport makes it very easy to produce good-looking reports, you can take full control of the content and layout of your report by using the Report Wizard. The Wizard includes the following reporting components:

- **Sorting**: You can apply single or multiple criteria sorts to the information that you want to include in your reports.

For example, if a business wanted to print a report on its customers, it could sort the information in order of (descending) sales value within (ascending) region name.

- **Grouping**: An elegant way of producing sorted reports is to group the records within the sort criteria.

  In the example of the customer report, Access would print the region name only once (and not on every line), and perhaps highlight the region name to make the report easier to read.

  When you group your data in this way, you can tell Access to perform calculations on the data within each group.

- **Layout**: Your options include Columnar (each included field on a separate line) and Tabular (each included record on a single line).

- **Style**: Options range from the plain (adequate for most purposes) to the very decorative (for marketing purposes, perhaps).

Grouped report

A report in which information is divided into easy-to-read blocks, with data sorted within each block. Calculations may be performed on the data within each block.

The best way to learn about the Access Report Wizard is to use it. Exercise 6.2 takes you through the steps.

Exercise 6.2: Producing a report with the Report Wizard

1 On the Database window, click the Reports icon, and then click the New button.

```
Design View
Report Wizard
AutoReport: Columnar
AutoReport: Tabular
Chart Wizard
Label Wizard
```

2 Select the Report Wizard, and specify that you want to produce a report based on the Birds table. Click **OK**.

3 Recognize the next screen? Yes, it's similar to the one you used to create tables and forms.

```
Birds
```

```
Tables/Queries
Table: Birds

Available Fields:              Selected Fields:
Number                         Bird Name
Colour                         Date Seen
Number Seen                    Place Seen
Migratory?
Size
Comments
```

Select the fields for inclusion in the report as shown. When finished, click the **Next** button.

4 How do want the records grouped in your report? You could, for example, produce a report for each bird, showing when and where you saw it. This would group together all the sightings of a given bird.

For this exercise, we'll produce a report by date. This will group together all sightings made on the same date. So select Date Seen and click the > button.

Click the **Grouping Options** button. You can group the sightings by year, quarter, month, week, day, and so on.

Group-level fields:	Grouping intervals:
Date Seen	Month ▾

Accept the default of Month and click OK. Click the **Next** button.

5   How do you want Access to sort the records in your report? Select Date Seen as the first sort criterion. The Sort button is initially set to sort ascending. To change the order, just click the button: each time you click it, it switches between ascending and descending. Make it descending. This means that your report will show the most recent sightings first.

1	Date Seen ▾	⬆
2	Bird Name ▾	⬇

Select Bird Name as the second sort criterion, and make it ascending. This means that the report will show the most recent sightings first, and on any given day it will show the birds sighted in alphabetical order. Click the **Next** button.

6 Select the layout for the report. As in previous Wizard exercises, you can get a good idea of what the final result will look like by selecting each in turn. Select the options as shown, and click the **Next** button.

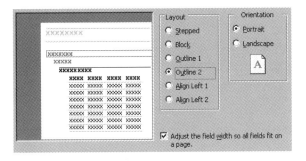

7 Select the typographic style for the report. Again, see what they look like by selecting them in turn.

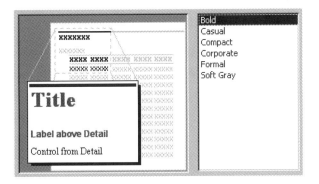

For the exercise, select Bold, and click the Next button.

8 Finally, give the report a title: Spotting Record. Select the Preview option, and click the **Finish** button.

After a few seconds, you see your report on screen. If it is exactly what you want, click the Print button on the toolbar, or choose **File | Print**. (The order in which the birds are listed depends in part on the data you chose to enter in Exercise 5.5.)

When finished, you can close your report.

Example of a report produced from Report Wizard

If there are birds without any details in their Place Seen and Date Seen fields, they are listed first at the top of the report. How would you create a report containing only birds that you have actually spotted? Answer: create and save a query that found only birds with a value in the Place Seen field, and then base the report on the query rather than the table.

Modifying the report layout

If the report produced by the Report Wizard does not meet your requirements exactly, you may want to fine-tune it. For example, the report you created in Exercise 6.2 needs to be tidied up a little. The range of possibilities in Access is very wide: we'll confine ourselves to a few.

In Exercise 6.3 you will format and change the size and position of some of your report's fields.

Exercise 6.3: Formatting the fields of a report

1 Open in Design view the report you created in Exercise 6.2. (To do this, at the Database window, select the Reports icon, select the Spotting Record report, and then double-click the Design button.)

2 The different elements in your report are shown against a grid. Each field has a title and a textbox. You can change the content or formatting of these in the same way as you did when you were designing a form (Exercise 5.6).

   Double-click in the label boxes listed below, and edit them as follows:

Before	After
Date Seen by Month	Month
Date Seen	Date

3 Click the text box for Month, and then click the Bold button on the toolbar.

4 Your next step is to reposition and increase the size of the three reports fields, so that they fill the width of the printed page.

   Click on the Place Seen title, and move the cursor anywhere over a border except on one of the handles. The cursor changes to an 'open hand' shape.

Drag the title about two centimetres to the right. Repeat this action for the Place Seen textbox.

Click on the Bird Name title and move the cursor to the sizing handle at the centre of its right border. The cursor changes shape to a double-headed arrow.

Drag the border about one centimetre to the right. Repeat this action for the Bird Name textbox.

5 Click the arrow to the right of the View button on the toolbar, and choose **Print Preview** to inspect your work. Close your report, saving your changes as you do.

Report sections

An Access report can contain five main sections, four of which are headers or footers, while the fifth is the actual body of the report itself. Let's look at each in turn:

- **Report Header and Footers**: Access prints these only once: at the start and at the end of the report respectively.

- **Page Header and Footers**: Access prints these at the top and at the bottom of every page.

  If a report includes a report header, Access prints the page header *after* it on the first page. If a report includes a report footer, Access prints the page footer *after* it at the bottom of the last page of the report.

- **Group Header and Footers**: User-defined groups can have their own headers and footers, which appear before and after the grouped data.

  Typically, the group header displays the values of the field that the group is defined on, and the group footer is used to create sub-totals of values within the group.

- **Report Details**: This is the part of a report that contains the information, drawn from a table or query, that you are reporting on. This section contains as many lines as there are records in the table or query.

In Design View, sections are represented as bands, and each section that the report contains is shown once.

Report sections in Design view

On the printed report, however, some sections may be repeated many times. In Exercise 6.4, you will edit the report header.

Exercise 6.4: Working with the Report Header and Footer

1 Open in Design view the report you worked on in Exercise 6.3.

2 In the Report Header section, click in the textbox containing the words 'Spotting Report'. You can now edit or delete the header text.

3 Change the text to 'Birdwatching Database'. Enlarge the text box to accommodate the text.

4 Click the arrow to the right of the View button on the toolbar, and choose **Print Preview** to inspect your work. Close your report, saving your changes as you do.

As you have learnt, the page header and footer appear under the Report Header on page 1, and at the top of every page in your report

Exercise 6.5: Working with the Page Header and Footer

1 Open in Design view the report you worked on in Exercise 6.4.

2 Move the mouse pointer slowly over the line dividing Page Header and Date Seen Header – it becomes a moving tool.

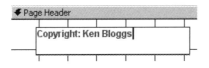

Click, hold and drag the Date Seen Header bar
down to make room between it and the
Page Header.

Toolbox button

3 Click the Toolbox button to display the Toolbox toolbar,
and on that toolbar click the Label button.

4 Move the cursor over the Page Header area.
Notice how the cursor changes shape.
Click where you want to position the
top-left corner of the textbox, hold down the
mouse button, drag the pointer to where the
bottom-right corner should be, and
release the mouse button.

Aa

Label button

$+ \text{A}$

Cursor shape for
drawing textboxes

5 Type the following text into the newly
created textbox: Copyright: Your Name.

```
◆ Page Header
  Copyright: Ken Bloggs|
```

You've now created a page header.

6 In the Page Footer area, click the left textbox that
contains 'Now()'. This is Access code for today's date.
Click the arrow to the right of the Font Color button on
the toolbar, and select the colour red.

7 In the Page Footer area, click the right textbox. Click the
arrow to the right of the Fill Color button on the
toolbar, and select the colour yellow.

8 Click the arrow to the right of the View button on the toolbar, and choose **Print Preview** to inspect your work.

9 Not happy with your colour choices? Return to Design view and make some further changes. When finished, close your report, saving your changes as you do. Close the Report Design dialog box.

Well done. You can close your Birds table and close Access. You have completed the *Databases* module of ECDL.

Chapter summary: so now you know

A *database report* is a document (printed or on screen) that presents information in a structured way. Access provides two automated solutions – *AutoReport* and the *Report Wizard* – that will satisfy most reporting requirements.

AutoReport offers two reporting options: *columnar*, in which Access prints each selected field on a separate line with the field name to its left, and *tabular*, where the fields of each record are printed on a single line and field names are printed once at the top of each page of the report.

To use the Report Wizard, choose the relevant table, select the fields you want to include, and specify the *grouping*, the *sort order*, the *layout* options and the presentation *styles*.

Grouping is an elegant way of producing sorted reports, as information is divided into easy-to-read blocks, with data sorted within each block.

An Access report can contain five main sections, four of which are headers or footers, while the fifth is the actual body of the report itself. The *Report Header* and *Report Footer* are each printed only once, at the start and at the end of the report respectively. At the top and bottom of every page Access can print a *Page Header* and *Page Footer*. Any user-defined groups can have their own *Group Header* and *Group Footer*. Finally, the *Report Detail* section contains the information, drawn from a table or query, that you are reporting on. This section contains as many lines as there are records in the table or query.

You can modify a report by changing the content of each field's title and textbox, by adjusting their size and position, and by applying formatting such as font, font colour and fill (background) colours.

You can insert or amend *headers* and *footers* to the report as a whole or to each page.